THE SABBATICAL GUIDEBOOK

THE NUTS, BOLTS, AND EVERYTHING ELSE YOU NEED TO PLAN YOUR SABBATICAL ADVENTURE

MATTHEW SAWASY

Copyright © 2022 by Matthew Sawasy

All rights reserved. No part of this book may be reproduced in any form or by any electronic or mechanical means, including information storage and retrieval systems, without written permission from the author, except for the use of brief quotations in a book review.

Disclaimer:
I am not a healthcare professional. All health-related content in this book should be considered as informational and for educational purposes only. Do not take anything here as medical advice. Always seek the advice of your doctor or other qualified health provider regarding anything health-related that you read or hear.

For my family and friends.
*Thank you all for supporting me
in making this book a reality.*

TABLE OF CONTENTS

Introduction	vii
THE IDEA	1
What is a sabbatical?	2
Who should take a sabbatical?	6
Why take a sabbatical?	7
Will a sabbatical impact my career negatively?	12
THE PLANNING	13
The best time to take a sabbatical	13
Important considerations when planning for a sabbatical	15
What to do on a sabbatical?	18
Sabbatical Types	22
Valuable activities for any sabbatical	28
How long should my sabbatical be?	31
How much will it cost?	32
How do I pay for my sabbatical?	36
What can I do with my stuff?	38
How can I sell my employer on the idea if my job doesn't offer sabbaticals?	40
What to do after my sabbatical?	42
How do I account for the gap in my resume?	45
What if something goes wrong during my sabbatical?	46
THE ACTION	51
Go for it	51
THE GROWTH	53
What does life look like after a sabbatical?	53
Considerations	55

YOUR QUICK SABBATICAL ESCAPE PLAN	57
MY LATEST SABBATICAL STORY	59
Europe	59
Thailand	63
Conclusion	67
Bibliography	69
About the Author	77

INTRODUCTION

> It does good also to take walks out of doors, that our spirits may be raised and refreshed by the open air and fresh breeze: sometimes we gain strength by driving in a carriage, by travel, by change of air, or by social meals and a more generous allowance of wine.
>
> SENECA

There is no magic to taking a sabbatical, but there is magic in taking a sabbatical. In fact, taking a sabbatical is just about the best choice you can make to gain a new perspective on this thing called life. There is an entire world outside your daily routine, beckoning you to explore it and enjoy its riches in the form of unforgettable experiences. You'll return to your life a changed person, but you'll be enriched, energized, and content.

This book draws on my own experiences, as well as the experiences of those with whom I have spoken about their sabbaticals, to give you a clear picture of what you can expect on your first

INTRODUCTION

extended break from work. You'll gain a comprehensive understanding of the concept of taking a sabbatical, what is involved financially, how you can structure your sabbatical, and what to do when it is time to return to your "normal" life.

In the fall of 2014, after spending 15 years immersed in the technology sector, my mind had had enough. Burnt-out, I decided to take a sabbatical. Other than taking a break from work, I really had no idea what a sabbatical entailed. Eight months later, I joined a new company, full of vigor and ready to give my all again.

Or so I thought.

Barely a year later, it dawned on me that I had made a mistake. The burnout from before my break had not dissipated at all, and the same feelings of frustration, discouragement, and lack of pleasure in my work seemed worse than before.

Two things were clear: I needed a longer sabbatical, and I needed a different kind of sabbatical. So, in between my work and social life, I started planning. In the winter of 2016, I left my job and sold all my possessions. When spring arrived, I hit the road for what turned into two of the best and most fulfilling years of my life.

While planning and taking my career breaks, I learned many unexpected things about myself, my friends and family, and about the process of taking a sabbatical. While on my third sabbatical, I had the realization that I should write down my findings and experiences to share them with others who need a break.

Whether you are planning a gap year, sabbatical year, or a career break, you will get something from this book.

Back when I took my second sabbatical, there weren't many resources available to explain the concept. In my search to better understand it, I only found a few books and blog posts. However, I was fortunate enough to have a family member who had started her retirement around the same time I started my sabbatical. Excited, we shared notes on our experiences of being away from the work environment, and I asked her what the first six to twelve months of her retirement life was like. During our chats, I found a lot of overlap between taking a sabbatical and entering retirement. I also took some time to talk with fellow workers who suffered from burnout and took sabbaticals as counter measures.

In my research, I discovered that most information on sabbaticals is geared toward educators in universities. Many universities have structured sabbatical systems in place that go back over one hundred years. Indeed, universities did not invent the concept of taking a sabbatical, but they were among the first institutions in the modern era to adopt the system.

That said, more and more people who are not university educators have now become interested in sabbaticals. From personal experience, I believe sabbaticals are an absolute must in the rushed world we live in. All of us need time to take a break and reconnect with ourselves, so we can feel our best and give our best during the times we participate in our communities through the work we do. Hopefully, this book will give some structure to those without the structured sabbatical systems offered by universities. For the most part, this book is as nuts and bolts as possible. As I work in a technical field, I like concise documentation, and, as such, will try to provide that here, all while giving you the tools you need to successfully embark on your first sabbatical.

While reading, keep in mind that career breaks are a very personal thing. What I planned, accomplished, and experienced on my career breaks could differ 100 percent from your career break. This book is not a step-by-step roadmap; instead, it is a guide intended to foster ideas in your mind for planning your sabbatical.

Before you continue, please take note that I claim no responsibility for any misfortune, misadventure, financial problems, acts of God, or Godzillas that may befall you before, during, or after your sabbatical.

THE IDEA

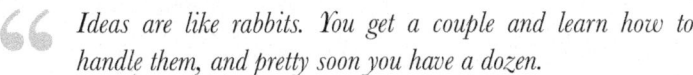 *Ideas are like rabbits. You get a couple and learn how to handle them, and pretty soon you have a dozen.*

JOHN STEINBECK

Few people will tell you this, but you should know that your first extended break from working will not always go smoothly. However, I can promise that you'll learn amazing things about the process, encounter like-minded people, and—most importantly—learn about yourself.

You should always have a plan, and I'll tell you why on page 14. But, above all, be flexible and let things happen without getting caught up in negative thought-cycles.

In the same way you have to learn which ideas that pop into your head are useful and worth pursuing, you have to learn the art of taking sabbaticals and figure out what works and doesn't work for you. This is a journey, after all.

WHAT IS A SABBATICAL?

The Short:

In this day and age, "sabbatical" is a much broader term than what it used to be when it was first conceptualized. While some may try to put what a sabbatical is (and is not) into a box, I believe the only one who can truly define it is you. At the end of the day, a sabbatical is whatever you want it to be.

The Long:

Simply put, a sabbatical is taking a break from your work, education or job. Traditionally, the practice of taking a break from work was reserved for people in academia. However, around the time of the dot-com bubble, the idea of career breaks seems to have gained wider acceptance in the collective mind. Anecdotal evidence indicates it was the new rich taking advantage of the time they now had to go and find themselves.

For example, Cecilia Pagkalinawan, who was known as 'The Internet Expert' in the early to mid 1990s, took off on a road trip with a couple of friends after the dot-com bubble had burst. During that time, they took a sabbatical and drove across the USA and experienced many adventures, all while contemplating their lives up to that point and figuring out what to do next.

Another dot-com entrepreneur, Ben Way, started taking sabbaticals shortly after the dot-com crash. He is a firm believer in how steering your mind away from business has significant benefits, like generating new ideas and returning to your work with renewed energy.

In the introduction, I alluded to the fact that the idea of a sabbatical goes back much further than modern academia. In the Jewish faith, there is the idea of *Shmita*, roughly translated as the "year of release" or "sabbatical year." This is the idea of taking a break from work in the seventh year of the seven-year agricultural cycle. The details of this "year of release" is outlined in the Torah and the Christian Bible, both in Leviticus Chapter 25 and Exodus Chapter 23.

The Ancient Greeks and Romans employed the concept of *Otium*. It is much more vaguely defined than *Shmita*, and can mean various things depending on context, but its essence is free time away from activity, or simply enjoying leisure time. In that sense, it can refer to an extended time away from work, like a sabbatical, a short vacation, or even retirement.

The modern-era idea of a sabbatical originated at Harvard University in 1880. After seven years of teaching, professors could take one year off and still receive half of their salaries. While I have no evidence that this is the original reason, research suggests sabbaticals are a way for educators to come down from their ivory towers and get a grounding in the world outside of academia.

Looking at more recent history, it seems that Intel was the first Silicon Valley company that offered sabbaticals to their employees. In fact, this is still one of their main "selling points" to new employees today.

All things considered, the idea of *Otium* seems to line up best with my idea of what a sabbatical is; that is: <u>whatever you want it to be</u>.

Different Terms, Same Thing?

The more you interact with people who are considering taking sabbaticals, even those who have been doing it for a long time, the more you'll hear terms like "career break," "sabbatical," and "gap year" being used interchangeably. You might be wondering whether there is a difference, so let's explore each concept on its own merit.

What is a sabbatical?

The word 'sabbatical' comes from the Latin word *sabbaticus*. It, in turn, comes from the Ancient Greek word σαββατικός (*sabbatikós*).

Cambridge Dictionary defines 'sabbatical' as: *a period of time when college or university teachers are allowed to stop their usual work in order to study or travel, usually while continuing to be paid.*

Collins Dictionary defines 'sabbatical' *as: a period of time during which someone such as a university teacher can leave their ordinary work and travel or study.*

What is a career break?

Cambridge Dictionary defines 'career break' as: *a period of time when you choose not to have a job, for example because you want to travel or take care of your children.*

Collins Dictionary defines 'career break' as: *If someone takes a career break, they stop working in their particular profession for a period of time, with the intention of returning to it later.*

What is a gap year?

Cambridge Dictionary defines 'gap year' as: *a year between leaving school and starting university that is usually spent traveling or working.*

Collins Dictionary defines 'gap year' as: *a period of time during which a student takes a break from studying after they have finished school and before they start college or university.*

So, what's the difference?

From the above definitions, you may conclude that one is exclusive to educators, another to students, and the last to people in the workforce. In essence, though, there is no difference between them—other than semantics.

In the rest of the book, I'll use the term 'sabbatical.' While, by its modern definition, it is for educators, the term is much older. Besides, the intention remains the same.

Is it a vacation?

For most people, time away from work, no matter how long, translates into a vacation. In light of this, it's natural to wonder if a sabbatical is just a long vacation with another name. Let's explore its definition to see if there is a difference.

Cambridge Dictionary defines 'vacation' as: *a holiday.*

Collins Dictionary defines 'vacation' as: *a period of time during which you relax and enjoy yourself away from home.*

If we compare definitions, it seems a sabbatical can include a vacation. However, a vacation is not a sabbatical. The further you investigate sabbaticals and learn more about them, you'll realize that a sabbatical, if planned properly, typically has a clearly-defined goal that results in personal growth and fulfillment. While a sabbatical can start off with a longer-than-usual vacation, it rarely ends up being a vacation in its entirety. In comparison, the only goal you have when taking a vacation is to relax and take a short break from your work environment.

Speaking of terminology

While writing this book, it became clear that there isn't a widely accepted term for someone who takes a sabbatical. 'Sabbitan,' 'sabbaticant,' and 'sabbatee' are a few of the terms I've encountered in my research. Throughout the book, I'll use the term 'sabbatee' for someone who is either taking a sabbatical or has done so already.

WHO SHOULD TAKE A SABBATICAL?

The Short:

Everyone, including you.

The Long:

While corporate America took almost a hundred years to catch up with universities in offering their employees extended breaks, it certainly spread like wildfire once it happened. Some say McDonald's was the very first 20th-century company to offer sabbaticals. However it started, the idea soon spread to legal, medical, and some government professions. After the dot-com bubble burst in 2001, sabbaticals became especially popular in the technology sector.

The dot-com bubble burst shifted the idea that sabbaticals could only be granted by employers on their terms. Burnt-out from the fast pace created by the bubble and its eventual collapse, many technology industry professionals took it on themselves to simply take a break, fund it themselves, and return to the workforce in their own time.

Now, more than ever, sabbaticals are within reach for 'normal' people like us. You need not be a high-earning executive to do it (most people I know who take sabbaticals aren't, and neither am I). All you need is the will to do it and the ability to plan, which we'll talk about later. With all the personal growth and fulfillment sabbaticals offer, everyone—even you—can benefit from taking time away from their day-to-day life.

WHY TAKE A SABBATICAL?

The Short:

Sabbaticals give you the opportunity to avoid (or recover from) burnout, test out retirement, and self-reflect.

The Long:

In 2002, Benshoff and Spruill asked 138 educators what they thought were the benefits of taking sabbaticals. The recurring personal benefits that came up in the study included the following:

- Self-care and rejuvenation
- Self-exploration
- Travel
- Creativity and exploring new ideas
- Time to focus on personal interests
- Time with family
- Respite from work

I, along with 33 percent of the respondents, found the rejuvenating effect of a sabbatical to be a key benefit. Whenever I take a sabbatical, it allows me to step off of my work treadmill and check in on myself. It gives me the chance to ask the question few people ask themselves:

"How am I doing?"

If you take a moment to answer that question, you will discover the reason you need a sabbatical. Heck, if we're being honest here, you probably knew the answer before you picked up this book!

Along with the crucial question of your wellbeing, you can ask yourself many more related questions, such as:

- How am I faring in my career?
- What would the 5-year-old me think of my life?
- How about the 12-year-old me?
- Am I working to survive, or am I working to live?
- How are my relationships?
- Am I achieving my life goals?
- What improvements can I make in my life?

The last question leads into, what I believe, is the greatest reason to take a sabbatical: <u>redesigning your life.</u> But before you can redesign, you have to take stock of where you are now to see the current design of your life. The only way to truly understand the current design of your life is to ponder over questions like the ones mentioned above. A sabbatical will give you the time, energy, and mental space to do just that.

Just from scanning over the above questions, you can probably already identify areas of your life you'd like to improve. Imagine what that end state (your redesigned life) would look like. With that end state in mind, you can begin to break down your goal and work backward to where you are now. You can think of this approach as building blocks or steps toward your ideal life. Now that you have laid out those steps, you will naturally start making decisions that align with your aspirations in order to achieve them. Congratulations, you are now redesigning your life.

If Lifestyle Design is a new concept for you, I highly recommend you invest in books and resources that specialize in the topic to learn about it as much as you can. The following books are popular starting points:

- *Designing Your Life: How to Build a Well-Lived, Joyful Life* by Bill Burnett and Dave Evans
- *The 4-Hour Workweek* by Tim Ferris

- *The Art of Non-Conformity: Set Your Own Rules, Live the Life You Want, and Change the World* by Chris Guillebeau

Lifestyle Design centers on designing your life around what is important to *you* instead of living a life designed by the culture and society you grew up in. By learning about Lifestyle Design, you can start living with purpose and gain the skills and mental tools that will give you the freedom to choose how you live your life. I recommend that you read up on Lifestyle Design before going on your sabbatical. Doing so will allow you to think of its importance and give you a foundation to build on when you have the mental space to start thinking about how you will redesign your life.

Aside from the above reasons for taking a sabbatical, your motivation could be whatever it is you want to do or achieve when you take that break. Whether you need to reflect on the direction your life is headed in, or whether you have an amazing idea in mind that you want to realize, the possibilities are endless.

Let's explore two more important reasons for taking a sabbatical.

Burnout

Of course, it's possible your desire to take a sabbatical is to recover from physical, mental, or emotional exhaustion related to your job. This type of exhaustion, better known as burnout, is one of the top reasons people take sabbaticals (and why some companies offer them).

Research on burnout is ongoing, and there are many theories as to what causes it and how it can be mitigated. Some experts even disagree on whether work is a cause for burnout at all. Expert opinions aside, most fellow workers I have had conversations with agreed wholeheartedly that their extreme exhaustion and eventual lack of motivation to get up in the morning and go to work was directly related to work itself. In fact, burnout was the reason I took my break back in 2014.

At any rate, taking a break from your career to recover from or prevent burnout is a great reason to take a sabbatical. The following signs are typical indicators that you are either burnt out already, or headed there faster than you think.

- Loss of interest in most to all aspects of your work.
- Everything about your job frustrates you intensely.
- You're struggling to think of anything outside of your work.
- Feelings of extreme exhaustion and difficulty sleeping.
- Loss of interest in your favorite activities and hobbies.
- Not being productive anymore.

Testing out retirement

Retirement is inevitable. While some of us are looking forward to it, others are dreading it. Regardless of which camp you are in, taking a sabbatical to test out retirement is an excellent idea.

If the idea of retirement makes you feel uneasy, taking a sabbatical will give you the opportunity to explore what it is about retirement you are not looking forward to. According to research done by Charles Schwab Investment Management Inc, the biggest fears people have around retirement are financial concerns. A sabbatical is a great way to see if the numbers in the real world work the same as they do on paper. While you won't have the passive income from the government or access to your retirement funds, you'll be able to see how your expenses work without the expectation of a salary to cover those expenses.

Maybe you're more concerned about the prospect of not knowing what to do with yourself when it's time to retire. Taking a break from work will motivate you to consider the available options. In most cases, I believe uneasiness about retirement comes down to an unconscious fear of the unknown. As humans, we are naturally more inclined to experiment and take on adventures when we have a better understanding of what to expect. A sabbatical will give you the test-run you need to enter the unknown and get a taste of what you can expect from retirement. Who knows, you might change your mind and even become excited about the idea.

Of course, if you are looking forward to retirement, I don't think I need to sell you on the idea of a career break.

In recent years, there has been a movement of people aggressively working toward Financial Independence and Retiring Early (FIRE). If you are following this principle but feel uncertain about leaving the working world behind, taking a sabbatical is a safe way to test out if the finances work out and whether the lifestyle suits you. In this case, it might be worth your while to negotiate with your employer for time off to take a sabbatical. That way, you'll have the security of a job to go back to while you test out the idea

There is conventional wisdom that we should build a life that we want to retire into. When applying the principles you'll learn from the concept of Lifestyle Design, there is no reason you can't build that life. Taking a sabbatical is a chance to see how you behave when you unplug and step off your own work treadmill. It is the best way to check in on your mental picture of retirement and to change or add goals for that time of your life.

As you can see, there are many reasons to take a sabbatical. It is, however, very personal to you. Your reason is also nobody else's business, so don't feel obligated to explain yourself to those who do not share your space. However, if you have a partner or dependants, it is fair to share your plans with them, as your decision will affect their lives.

WILL A SABBATICAL IMPACT MY CAREER NEGATIVELY?

The Short:

It depends on your industry and experience.

The Long:

Taking a sabbatical will probably not set you back in your career. But there are some considerations and caveats involved when choosing to take one.

The biggest factor, I would say, is the competitiveness of the industry you work in. Along with that, you need to consider how long you have been working. For example, I work in the technology sector, which is quite competitive. However, by the time I took my second sabbatical, I had 15 years of experience. Personally, my time away from the industry had no effect on my career at all.

There are ways to avoid gaps on your resume, like negotiating for a sabbatical with your employer. In that case, you will technically still be employed and there will be no need to indicate your time away from work, no matter how long you were away from the office.

On the other hand, a sabbatical can impact your career positively. From a potential employer's point of view, knowing that you took time off to pursue a hobby related to your work might count in your favor.

Distancing yourself from your career and industry will give you the time to think about the coming years. You can gain new perspectives on what you want to do and achieve, and this can be a positive thing for your professional and personal development.

THE PLANNING

 If you fail to plan, you are planning to fail!

BENJAMIN FRANKLIN

THE BEST TIME TO TAKE A SABBATICAL

The Short:

Your sabbatical should not become a source of stress, so only take one when you can afford it financially and professionally.

The Long:

There really is no right or wrong time to take a sabbatical, assuming all is well in your life. When you take your sabbatical is just as personal as the reason for taking it. I always say it's better to take a sabbatical before you *need* one, but an overdue sabbatical is better than no sabbatical at all.

As with most ventures in life, there are many reasons you can come up with not to take a sabbatical. However, when you think about it, the major issue always comes down to money. If you can make the money work, you can address and find solutions for all the other reasons with more ease. We'll address many of these concerns throughout the book. Money is indeed the one factor that can make or break your prospective sabbatical, but it is not impossible to save up enough to make it happen. In the "How much will it cost?" section of the book (page 30), I'll tell you about the nuts and bolts of the financial aspect. Once you get a better idea of how it works, your perception of how achievable it is to take a sabbatical may change.

While this is a personal and subjective statement, I feel that sabbaticals find us. What I mean is that most, if not all, people daydream about quitting their jobs or retirement, but few actually investigate taking time away from work. On the other hand, those who think about sabbaticals usually follow through (this has been the case with almost everyone I have talked with during my research).

The fact that you are here, reading this book, tells me that a sabbatical has already found you—whether you've already taken it or not.

Since sabbaticals are typically 3 to 12 months, it is wise to plan ahead. Friedman (2018) suggests taking two years to plan, especially if you're going to move or travel with your family. Experience has taught me this is a good amount of time to plan, as it can result in an amazing sabbatical. This is roughly the same length of time I had spent planning my latest and most wondrous sabbatical.

For example, I was able to spend a year eating my way across every country in Western Europe, track down my great grandfather's resting place in France, haunt every major museum along the way, and many, many more personal goals. Looking back, this sabbatical was very different from my first attempt at a career break in the fall of 1997. I was a few years out of high school, working in the service industry, and had no idea what I wanted to do in life. As was common with my peers, I left for Australia to backpack around and find myself. I spent months bumming around from city to city, sometimes following the fruit harvests to make money picking fruit. It was fantastic to travel and backpack at that age and at that time.

It changed the way I looked at the world, and, while I didn't find myself, I knew what I wanted to do next.

IMPORTANT CONSIDERATIONS WHEN PLANNING FOR A SABBATICAL

Money

"Money makes the world go round" may feel like a cliché, but it is an apt saying in a world where we need money to survive and thrive. If you want time away from generating money, you still need enough of it to enjoy yourself without worrying about your finances.

When you can take a sabbatical really comes down to when you can support yourself and how it will impact you financially. The chapter on *How much will it cost?* digs into what you need to take time away from work.

Career

As discussed in the previous section, *Will it impact my career negatively?*, it is worth taking some time to think about where you are in your career.

Some people love what they do and cannot imagine another career path. In that case, you need to be very sure that you are in a place in your career where you can take a break without negative consequences when you return to the workforce. Much like the Harvard sabbatical program specifies, I would suggest that you have spent at least seven years on your current career path. This will ensure that you have experience to offer when you're ready to work again. If you do not have seven years of experience, I would caution you to stay on a little longer for your own sake. When you start planning for your sabbatical, talk with the HR department to see if your company offers sabbaticals. That way, you will have the security of your existing job when you return and not risk a gap in your CV. If your company does offer sabbaticals, stay in touch with the HR department and your supervisor or manager to make sure you consider and attend to all work-related commitments before you take your break.

On the other hand, there are people who are not so sure they've chosen the right career or industry. If you have been working in the same industry for five years or less and are already frustrated, discouraged, and find little to no joy in what you do, these might be tell-tales that you have not yet found your 'thing.' In that case, I suggest you plan your break around getting to know yourself better and identifying what it is you want to do in life. You might even discover that your environment, and not your chosen career path, was the culprit behind your displeasure. Taking a sabbatical early in your career is a risk in the sense that you might not get a job immediately after your return, but it is not impossible. As long as you can offer an employer value and provide a solid reason for that gap in your CV, you will be able to make things work in your favor.

Whatever your professional situation, be responsible in your planning and make sure you can sustain yourself (and whoever depends on you) during your sabbatical.

Family

If you have a partner, children, or other dependents, you'll need to consider how your sabbatical will affect them.

THE PLANNING 17

While each person's familial life is unique, there are general guidelines you can keep in mind while making plans. For example, if there is enough money to sustain everyone and your sabbatical does not include traveling or moving, the implications for your family will probably be small. However, if you do plan a move during your sabbatical, you'll need to consider your partner's career, the kids' school and summer breaks, and other aspects that may disrupt your family's normal rhythm. If you can identify the ways in which a sabbatical may change things in your household, you and your partner and dependents can brainstorm and talk about working around those changes.

Time

Chances are that you will not be satisfied with one sabbatical for the rest of your life. Once you experience the freedom and joy it adds to your existence, taking sabbaticals will most likely become a part of your life. When you think about it, taking sabbaticals is really a lifestyle. How often you'll take them is, of course, up to you. Your personal situation and finances will determine how you go about the planning when you consider the time factor.

A friend told me about a sabbatical idea that really piqued my interest. I call it the 5 year/1 year plan. It's a simple idea, but harder to implement. The idea is to work very hard for 5 years and save as much money as possible. After 5 years, you leave your job, sell your possessions, and travel for a year. There are ways to stretch your money during these sabbaticals, like setting up in a country with low living costs.

The nice thing about this sabbatical idea is that it puts your breaks on a schedule, motivating you to work toward that next sabbatical. It also means that you will take a sabbatical, whether you need one or not or not. Doing it this way comes with unique benefits, like the assurance that you can prevent work-related burnout and the excitement of working toward your next adventure.

Of course, the 5 year/1 year plan has drawbacks. It might not be the best option if you have children, as they require an education and cost a fair bit of money. Also, while not impossible, living this way makes buying a home or investing for retirement much more difficult. Another important consideration is that you need to be a disciplined person, willing to sacrifice a few things you would otherwise have invested in during your 5-year working sprint. Living this way means that most of your savings go toward the next sabbatical, so whether that works for you or not depends on your personality and what you value or consider a worthwhile and successful life. There is no right or wrong approach in this regard; you just need to do what works for *you*.

WHAT TO DO ON A SABBATICAL?

The Short:

Take a vacation at the start of your sabbatical. Other than that, do whatever you like, as long as you find value in how you spend your time.

The Long:

I would like to preface this section by saying that there is nothing wrong with doing nothing or going nowhere on a sabbatical. If you want to spend your free time at home, tending to the garden, painting rocks, meditating, or similar activities, there *is* value in that. *This is also a plan.*

However, for most people, the idea of taking a sabbatical is closely related to some goal, such as writing, doing volunteer work, or sailing. As we talked about earlier, it is important to spend time planning out what you would like to do on your sabbatical *before* it starts. In the beginning, I made the mistake of

THE PLANNING 19

thinking I would spend time at the start of my sabbatical to plan the rest of my sabbatical. The moment I stepped away from my job, though, I started sleeping long hours. Without my alarm, I slept 10 to 12 hours, and this was followed by me goofing around on the Internet or playing video games. That was about it.

Eventually, when started working on my sabbatical plans, it took much, much longer than I expected. In between catching up with lost sleep, goofing around, and working on my sabbatical plans, I wasted half of the eight months I had planned to take. Let me point out that "wasting time" is a relative term here. For me, it felt like I had wasted half of my sabbatical because I had something else in mind about what it was supposed to entail. That is not to say that if you want to spend your sabbatical at home in a similar manner, it would be time wasted for you. It is all about expectations, which is why planning is so crucial to make those expectations a reality.

The following ideas of how to spend a sabbatical are just suggestions. If anything, I hope they will re-ignite some long-forgotten desire within you and motivate you to start making plans to do that thing you have always wanted to do.

Take a vacation

If there is one take away from this book, I would say it is this: plan a vacation for the start of your sabbatical. Go lie on a sunny beach somewhere, camp in the wilderness, or ski a snow-capped mountain top. Whatever your idea of a vacation, make sure you escape to one.

Ideally, by the time you go on vacation, you should at least have come up with the broader strokes of what you'd like to accomplish with your sabbatical. So, spend some of your vacation time thinking about the finer details of what you want to do. Think of it as an opportunity to focus on the nuts and bolts. When you get back to your sabbatical, you'll have a more fleshed-out plan. On top of that, you will have switched your brain from work mode to just being you, ready to make the best of your free time without the hassles of trying to compete in the rat race.

Practice sleep hygiene

Sleep hygiene refers to the habits and behavior you practice with regards to sleep. Your sleeping environment also plays a role in sleep hygiene. Most people have a love-hate relationship with sleep. We know we need it (and secretly love it), but we treat it as an obstacle or daunting chore. The truth is, sleep is a very important factor in personal health. Without enough of it, your body and mind will eventually suffer and punish you for not taking care of yourself.

When planning your sabbatical, allow for a slow start. Give your body and mind time to recover from the stresses and schedule of your regular day-to-day. As I mentioned, I slept up to 12 hours a day on one of my sabbaticals. This was not mere laziness, it was my body claiming its sleep debt. If you sleep less than what your body needs, the lost need for rest does not disappear. Somehow, someday, you need to make up for it.

Since learning more about the importance of quality sleep, I've toyed with the idea of taking short breaks in my career, just to focus on sleep. I didn't pay enough attention to sleep until a psychologist forced me to do it. He refused to get into anything until I had my sleep sorted out. I thought it was a put-on, but it was three sessions before we talked about things other than sleep. By the third session, out of spite, I was following his recommendations. Happily, this is what started my passion for sleep hygiene.

Here is an excerpt from my journal focusing on sleep hygiene during a sabbatical:

THE PLANNING

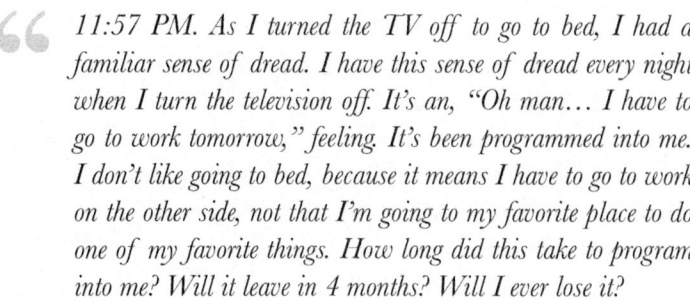

> *11:57 PM. As I turned the TV off to go to bed, I had a familiar sense of dread. I have this sense of dread every night when I turn the television off. It's an, "Oh man… I have to go to work tomorrow," feeling. It's been programmed into me. I don't like going to bed, because it means I have to go to work on the other side, not that I'm going to my favorite place to do one of my favorite things. How long did this take to program into me? Will it leave in 4 months? Will I ever lose it?*

Fortunately, and I should say surprisingly, it only took me a few nights to shake off that awful feeling and actually start to smile before bedtime. I'm also happy to say that it hasn't returned. Of course, I still get this feeling the night before having to do something I'd rather not; but, as a general rule, I am happy to head off to sleep at night.

I have also found it common for me to get a cold just after starting a sabbatical or taking a vacation. There are a few theories on why this is, such as the low constant stress from my job keeping me and my immune system in fight mode. Then, when I take time away from work, my stress levels drop and my immune system stands down, resulting in me getting sick. I have no science to back this reasoning up. Regardless, it's common for me to get sick, and I've talked to peers who experience the same thing, so I think it's worth mentioning there is a possibility of getting sick when you stop working. As I said at the beginning, be flexible and let things happen on your sabbatical.

Best Practices for Sleep Hygiene

The following tips will help you get started with forming healthy sleeping habits. It only touches the surface of practicing sleep hygiene, and I want to encourage you to read up on the science behind quality sleep. It will change your perception of sleep, as well as your relationship with it.

- Your bed is for sleeping only, so no reading, watching TV, eating, or working on your tablet or laptop.
- If possible, don't use an alarm clock. Let your body wake up naturally.
- If you can't fall asleep within 20 minutes, get out of bed and change your scenery. Go watch TV, write down your thoughts, or engage in any other activity.
- Train your mind by setting up indicators that it is bedtime. For example, I have my living room lights on a timer. When it's time for bed, they simply switch off.
- Practice meditation. When you experience difficulties falling asleep, it's because you haven't given your mind the space or time to process events from the day. You need not follow mainstream meditation practices. For example, if I spend 15 minutes a day listening to the sound of waves and stare at the wall, I fall asleep without difficulty at night.
- If you take naps, be sure they last no longer than 20 minutes. There are different techniques to make sure you stick to short naps, such as:
- The caffeine nap: drink coffee just before your nap to ensure high energy levels when you wake up.
- The spoon nap: hold a spoon or other object that can make a sound in one hand when you take your nap. You'll want the hand holding the spoon to rest off the edge of the bed. When you start drifting off into a deep sleep, your hand will relax and drop the spoon, waking you up.

SABBATICAL TYPES

The sky is the limit when it comes to choosing a type of sabbatical to take. As far as I know, there is no handbook out there to define types of sabbaticals, no set standard. It is your time to do what you want to do. You know you best! There is also no rule that says you have to focus on one thing during your sabbatical. That said, I do recommend it from personal experience. Some time after you have caught up on sleep and you start disconnecting from the schedule of your work, your perception of time will slow down. If the goal of your sabbatical is to relax and do nothing, this isn't really a problem. If you intend to accomplish things, it's good to be aware of this phenomenon and implement strategies around it, like taking that vacation at the start of your sabbatical.

Some will argue that some of the following aren't types of sabbaticals, but, like I said, there is no set standard to define which activities constitute sabbaticals. For example, you may hear that going to school, working, or taking parental leave are not sabbaticals. I disagree. We've already established that 'sabbatical' is a very loosely defined term and, essentially, it's about taking time away from your career for whatever reason.

With that said, here are some of the most popular types of sabbaticals people take:

Travel

This one is a classic. Whether living out of a backpack, cruising in a motorhome, or jet-setting between cities, there is so much to learn on a travel sabbatical. From a young age, I have always equated travel with education. When I was backpacking in my twenties, I realized it was really another form of education. The wondrous things you see, the adventures you experience while traveling, the people you meet, the life and survival skills you learn… they all add up to an education that rivals structured education, at least in my opinion. As such, I place a lot of value on this sabbatical type.

While backpacking through Europe in 2017, I realized just how much work traveling takes. Going where the wind blows is exciting, but it can be an expensive way to travel. In Europe, I found that most modes of transport were cheaper when booking a couple of weeks ahead.

Traveling alone offered me the benefit of easy decisions. I could go wherever I wanted and whenever I wanted. Ironically, the downside was that all the decisions and planning were my responsibility. I spent whole afternoons sitting in hostels, looking at maps and travel websites, booking flights, trains rides, hostels, hotels, Airbnbs, bus rides, and car sharing.

I did rather enjoy the planning process, but it can be a bit daunting trying to keep ahead of the two weeks of travel 'runway.' Balancing tearing around a new town with planning your travel can be exhausting at times.

Of course, the few hassles and headaches that accompany a travel sabbatical are completely worth it. Spending my birthday sitting in a hot tub in a glass-roofed hotel spa, watching the icy wind blow clouds down the Andorran valley, is a memory I'll never forget.

Invest in your education and personal development

Furthering education or a research topic were part of the original intents of taking sabbaticals for educators working at universities. That is because a sabbatical is a perfect opportunity to learn something new. Whether you want to further a hobby or passion project, advance your career by focusing on training, or educate yourself into a completely new career, a sabbatical is a great way to do so.

If this is the type of sabbatical you want to pursue, I would suggest investigating online courses, institutions to receive training, reliable mentors, and so on during your planning process, before your sabbatical starts. That way, you will not use up too much of your time researching. Instead, you'll be able to choose the best course of action from a short list of options much quicker and start your educational journey soon after your initial vacation.

Work

It may sound counterintuitive—who wants to work while taking a break from work, after all? But challenging your mind in another direction altogether will feel exciting and stimulate your ability to think creatively and broadly, instead of focusing on the narrow thinking pathways offered by most jobs.

'Work' need not equate to 'corporate.' Maybe you are an office worker who wants to help the environment by planting trees or joining an ocean clean-up crew for a summer. Or perhaps you're interested in joining the Red Cross for a while. On the other hand, your sabbatical may be the perfect opportunity to make the start-up you've been dreaming of launching a reality.

Research your roots

Travel to your ancestral homeland to investigate where your family came from. Perhaps this will involve brushing up on your familial language, too.

Write

If you have been picking away at a book for years, a writing sabbatical may be just the thing you need. Whether it's a future bestselling novel or a movie script idea that you need to pen down, you can write it from anywhere in the world. Why not find a remote location in the Alaskan wilderness and spend your days capturing your great ideas in solitude? Or do it on the beaches of Thailand, if that is where your inner writer will find inspiration.

Parental or family leave

Taking time away from your career to focus on your family is a worthy undertaking. If you want to spend more time at home to raise your child, help a sick loved one, or focus on the relationships with those you care about, I think it makes sense to approach it as a sabbatical and plan around that.

Volunteer

Spending most of your time at work and then resting to regain your energy over weekends or off days may give you the feeling that you aren't contributing to society as a whole. There are countless ways to volunteer during a sabbatical. You can help with anything from educating impoverished children, to helping at a science research station, to building houses in America.

The problem with this type of sabbatical is not finding volunteering opportunities, but picking the ones you wish to do!

Focus on you

While all sabbaticals will better you in one or more aspects of your life, some breaks focus more on this idea

Of all the "I need to focus on me" sabbaticals, the one I love most is the Yoga and Meditation Retreat. All the people I have talked with who retreated to India for six months (or more) to practice yoga have all said it was the best thing they could have done for themselves. This idea really resonates with me, and I hope to do it someday.

We all have heard people say they need a break from the rat-race. At its core, this is a classic cry for a "I need to focus on me" sabbatical.

This type of sabbatical is all about changing your routines and breaking your current day-to-day habits to reinvent yourself. Of

THE PLANNING 27

course, it is your sabbatical and you don't need to have some rigid structure or program in place. You can always take the time to do anything, like getting in touch with who you were before you started your career, joining a club to learn a new sport and improve your health, or taking transformative learning courses at your community college.

As I am very passionate about Sleep Hygiene these days, I have to mention it as part of this sabbatical type. I'm not sure I would devote an *entire* sabbatical to fixing my sleeping patterns, but that's just me. Of course, you are more than welcome to do just that if you want to—it is your sabbatical!

Go Sailing

While this is probably a niche sabbatical, I think it's common enough to mention. For humans, there is something magical and romantic about water, and the sea in particular.

Sailing has become a sought-after sabbatical activity. If you're the active type, it might just be the perfect way for you to spend your break. You can go on an extended sailing trip, or combine the activity with a travel sabbatical, where you go on shorter sailing trips in different countries.

Start or focus on a hobby, personal project, or side hustle

Taking time to focus on your hobby is another classic. Working on that classic car rebuild or finishing a woodworking project resonates with many people.

If you're bored with your current hobby, or don't have one at all, you can spend your time finding and learning a new one. Taking a cooking class at the community center, a sewing class at the community college, or watching knitting videos online are all worthwhile undertakings on your sabbatical. You may remember that I mentioned starting a new hobby as part of the *Invest in Your*

Education and Personal Development section. This is a classic example of how sabbatical types can overlap and meet each other, which is one of the reasons I believe no one should tell you which activities constitute sabbatical activities. As mentioned before, these are simply suggestions to ignite your creative spark.

In the same vein as starting a new hobby, you may want to get a side hustle off the ground. For those unfamiliar with the concept, a side hustle is work you do in addition to your main job to make extra money. Be mindful, though, that most side hustles require a lot of initial work before they start generating money on 'autopilot.'

Test the Digital Nomad lifestyle

Digital Nomadism is a lifestyle where practitioners undertake online work that is completely remote. This type of work allows them to live nomadically, moving from country to country as they wish.

One tip from my personal experience is to see if you can have work lined up before you start. It can be a little demoralizing trying to hustle up work versus working during this sabbatical.

Tick off a "bucket list" goal

All of us have a few things we really, really want to do before we kick the bucket. The only factors holding most people back from doing those things are time and freedom. A sabbatical, however, is a perfect opportunity to hike the Appalachian Trail, go swimming with sharks, or achieve whatever amazing idea you have.

VALUABLE ACTIVITIES FOR ANY SABBATICAL

Most people feel good when there is structure in their days. Personally, I am a goal-oriented person. Maybe this is you, too.

Maybe not. Either way, I think the following activities and habits are worth your consideration, regardless of the type of sabbatical you choose.

Keep a journal

Whether you want to write with a pen and paper, type something out electronically, or keep voice recordings on your phone, I highly recommend recording and saving your daily thoughts for the following reasons:

- You will probably have some wonder-filled days you'll want to remember.
- There is a lot you will learn about yourself while on your sabbatical.
- You will probably have excellent ideas as your mind decouples from work. Note them and come back to them at any point in the future.

In addition to keeping a journal to store your thoughts, I think a photo journal is also a neat idea. Take pictures of yourself every day or capture your wonderful experiences.

Talk with a life coach, counselor, or therapist

This is something I wish I had done at the start of my 2014 sabbatical, and that's why I recommend it. I spent many days feeling unhappy. The worst part was that I could not determine the root of my unhappiness. Some time later, I realized I was having trouble letting go of things at my job that weren't my problem anymore and having difficulty settling into being on sabbatical. I probably could have gone through this quicker if I had help.

Plan your days

While some of us need more structure than others, we all have this in common: we need goals to avoid unhealthy patterns. It is too easy to just watch TV, eat constantly, or sleep your days away. Don't get me wrong, I *highly* recommend all three activities, but you'll probably want to avoid spending your entire sabbatical doing them.

Having a simple, loose plan in place for a few days in advance will help you feel like you are spending your time wisely and that your days are fulfilling.

Exercise, or practice yoga or meditation

Regardless of what you do on your sabbatical, it pays to form new habits with activities that stimulate your body and mind. Exercising or practicing yoga and meditation will jumpstart your brain for whatever lies ahead that day. Apart from that, your body will thank you for taking better care of it by giving you fewer aches and pains.

Don't overload yourself

This tip ties in with the planning phase of your sabbatical.

As a counterpoint to all the wonderful ideas you have for your sabbatical, take a moment to think if what you hope to do is indeed achievable. Compile a list of all the things you hope to accomplish and then, with that list in mind, think about how much time you will take for your sabbatical. Scrutinize your ideas and narrow them down to fit into the time you'll have available. As mentioned earlier, your perception of time will change when you are away from your work schedule, so keep that in mind.

The best thing you can do now is cut that list in half. Seriously. From that new, smaller list, you'll probably accomplish about half of what you plan to do.

Once, before starting a sabbatical, I had created a list of the things I hoped to accomplish. My list contained around 30 to 40 items. In the end, I started half of them and accomplished about four things. That was over the course of eight months!

HOW LONG SHOULD MY SABBATICAL BE?

The Short:

Factors like whether you'll return to the same job, the length of time you can negotiate, your responsibilities, and your financial health will influence the period of your sabbatical.

The Long:

There is a bit to unpack in this question. For instance, are you planning on returning to the same job after your sabbatical ends? If so, the length of your sabbatical will likely be whatever you can negotiate with your employer. Unless you are employed at a university, you can expect your employer to give you paid time off for four weeks to three months, depending on how long you have been employed. If you want more time off, chances are a large chunk of your sabbatical will be unpaid (if you manage to negotiate a longer time than what your employer would normally grant). However, if you are planning on leaving your current job, your sabbatical can be whatever length you want, even open-ended.

Fixed length or open-ended?

The answer to this question depends on your personality.

For me, I had always left my jobs when my sabbaticals came around, so I had no fixed end date. My sabbaticals ran until I ran out of money, became homesick, or wanted to get back to working.

I know fellow sabbatical enthusiasts who have taken fixed length sabbaticals and thoroughly enjoyed it; however, they always had that end date in the back of their minds.

I think this is the trade-off: having the security of a job to go back to, or the freedom of being unencumbered. The answer to this question is, which of these is more important to you?

HOW MUCH WILL IT COST?

The Short:

Aside from what you need for the day-to-day of spending, it is worth considering what life will look like after your sabbatical. How much money will be left? And how fast can you start earning again?

The Long:

This question is probably the one most people will flip to, along with "*How do I pay for it?*"

The truth is that there is no one answer. It really depends on you and what type of sabbatical you want to take. Whatever the type of sabbatical you take, there are basic things you'll need:

- Shelter
- Food
- Transportation
- Communication
- Access to medical care

After the above needs, costs become more dependent on what activities will happen before or during the sabbatical. Considerations, for example, include:

- Sightseeing costs

THE PLANNING

- Leisure activity costs (a symphony, dining out, etc.)
- Schooling costs for your kids or your own educational development
- Entry visa costs
- Insurance costs
- Vaccination costs
- Possession storage costs

For someone like me, who lives a minimalist lifestyle and mostly goes on travel sabbaticals, the costs will be very different from a family of four planning the same trip. The volume of costs would be different, but also the way we travel. For example: I can cram into a full bus for 10 hours for a €9 trip from Paris to Toulouse. But a family with young children probably can't or won't do this.

The approach I recommend for understanding the costs your sabbatical will entail is to work backward. Here are some considerations:

- Decide what type of sabbatical you'll take.
- Decide what you'll do on the sabbatical.
- Determine how long your sabbatical will be.
- Take into account how many people will join you.

Once you know the above factors, it will be a matter of breaking down your sabbatical activities into smaller parts until you can correlate them to costs.

For example, let's assume a nuclear family wants to take a six-month sailing sabbatical through the South Pacific.

Here what their cost breakdown might look like:

RENTAL

ITEM	PRICE	TOTAL
Sailboat	$20,000 x 6 months	$120,000
Skipper Salary	$4,000 x 6 months	$24,000
Food Costs	$1,000 x 6 months	$6,000
Health Insurance	$2,000 x 4 people	$8,000
Boat Insurance	$300 x 6 months	$1,800
Flight to Fiji	$2,000 x 4 people	$8,000
Port/Mooring Fees	$400 x 90 days	$36,000
Hotel Fees (Transit)	$200 x 4 people	$800
Fuel Costs (Boat & Dinghy)	$200 x 6 months	$1,200
Visa Costs	$1,000	$1,000
Internet Costs	$150 x 6 months	$900
TOTAL		**$207,700**

PURCHASE

ITEM	PRICE	TOTAL
Sailboat	$360,000	$360,000
Sailing Lessons	$5,000	$5,000
Boat Registration	$5 x 40 feet	$200
Boat Maintenance	$1,000 x 6 months	$6,000
Food Costs	$1,000 x 6 months	$6,000
Health Insurance	$2,000 x 4 people	$8,000
Boat Insurance	$300 x 6 months	$1,800
Flight to Fiji	$2,000 x 4 people	$8,000
Port/Mooring Fees	$400 x 90 days	$36,000
Hotel Fees (Transit)	$200 x 4 people	$800
Fuel Costs (Boat & Dinghy)	$200 x 6 months	$1,200
Visa Costs	$1,000	$1,000
Internet Costs	$150 x 6 months	$900
TOTAL		**$434,900**

Once you have completed the cost breakdown exercise and have a rough number in mind of how much your sabbatical will cost, my advice is to add at least another twenty percent on top of that. Life happens. There is one event that always comes back to me when planning my own sabbatical budgets. During my 2014 sabbatical, after going to sleep the very first night as an unemployed sabbatee, I woke up with terrible tooth pain the next morning. Shortly thereafter, I had to have a root canal done. With each of my sabbaticals, many unexpected costs and events have always come up, and I have no doubt this will continue. My good advice to you is to protect yourself from these unexpected costs as best you can.

HOW DO I PAY FOR MY SABBATICAL?

The Short:

Save up, find a way to generate income independently of your regular job, or both.

The Long:

Perhaps the biggest concern for anyone who wants to go on a sabbatical is how to pay for it. There is no silver bullet answer to this. From what I've gathered through conversations with other sabbatees, there are many ways to go about financing a sabbatical.

There are numerous excellent books on personal finance and generating wealth, and it's indeed a vast topic that deserves an entire discussion on its own. Since that is not the goal of this book, we will not talk about the details. However, I will refer you to some excellent books to get you started below. After that, I want to give you a few pointers specific to sabbaticals.

THE PLANNING 37

- *The Total Money Makeover: Classic Edition: A Proven Plan for Financial Fitness* by Dave Ramsey
- *The Common Path to Uncommon Success: A Roadmap to Financial Freedom and Fulfillment* by John Lee Dumas
- *Financial Freedom: A Proven Path to All the Money You Will Ever Need* by Grant Sabatier

Create a savings account for your sabbatical

When you start thinking about taking a sabbatical, one of the first things you need to determine (even if it's a rough estimate) is the costs involved. When you know that, you can plan your finances around your future sabbatical.

Saving up money for this will require a lot of willpower and discipline. You might have to skimp on regular pleasures for a year or two. Whether or not you are willing to do this will depend on how motivated you are to enjoy total freedom when that sabbatical comes around. Not everyone is in a position to save up everything they'll need for their sabbatical, though, so they might need another financial source to make up the balance.

Sublet your home

Instead of giving up your home when going on a sabbatical, subletting it for some extra money might be a wiser option. However, you'll need to have a decent grasp of the law around this concept wherever you live. If this is something you want to consider, get your facts straight first.

Of course, if you are a homeowner, you have the option of letting your house for the time you'll be away.

Generate income during your sabbatical

Earlier, we touched on Digital Nomadism. This is not really a sabbatical type, but it is a viable option to generate money while you travel.

You might also consider getting that side hustle idea off the ground before you go on your sabbatical. If you manage to let it grow during the time you plan your sabbatical, there is a fair chance it could be generating some extra money by the time you take your break.

Request a Tax Break

Get in touch with a tax professional before your sabbatical. There might be certain benefits available to you during the time you won't be generating your regular income.

Crowdfunding

If approached right, crowdfunding is a legit way to make up the extra money you need for your sabbatical. I would say it depends on the type of sabbatical you're planning to take. If, for example, you plan on traveling, those who receive your request may feel that you want them to sponsor your holiday. As you can imagine, this will not sit well with most people. However, if you want to go plant trees, research an important topic like cancer, or volunteer to help those in need, people will most likely feel inclined to support your cause. Be sure to actually follow through on your plans, though.

WHAT CAN I DO WITH MY STUFF?

The Short:

Depending on your plans, you can consider different options:

- *Leave your stuff at home.*
- *Ask your friends or family to keep it safe.*
- *Sell everything.*
- *Donate everything.*
- *Put your stuff away in long-term storage.*

The Long:

If you are planning a travel sabbatical or any other activity that will require you to give up your living space, you'll naturally have to make a plan with your possessions.

If you are a homeowner, you can probably rent out your place furnished and make a plan with your personal and sentimental possessions. In this case, I would suggest devoting a lot of time to finding someone trustworthy to check up on and manage your property while you're away. Even then, there is some risk of damage involved, so you'll have to weigh the pros and cons and decide what's best for you.

Whether you are a homeowner or a tenant, the easiest solution, I believe, is to pack up your stuff and move them into long-term storage. You can achieve this by either paying for storage or reaching out to friends and family who might be kind enough to house your possessions while you travel. You can also use the opportunity to donate or sell that bunch of stuff you didn't even know you still have.

This is the route I took for my 2014 sabbatical. I got rid of everything, from my furniture to my car. Aside from some legal papers and a coin collection, everything I owned was in my backpack.

Of course, the above method will definitely not work for everyone. You need to do whatever makes you comfortable and makes the most sense to you.

Donating some of your things to charity will give them a new purpose and help others who may desperately need what you have. Although this should not be a primary motivator, I believe it's worth knowing that you might get some tax credit for your donations.

HOW CAN I SELL MY EMPLOYER ON THE IDEA IF MY JOB DOESN'T OFFER SABBATICALS?

The Short:

At the end of the day, any business wants productive employees that help move the bottom line along. As long as you offer value and show that a sabbatical will enable you to continue doing so in the long run, there is a good chance your employer will agree to grant a sabbatical.

The Long:

There are various reasons you may not want to quit your job when taking a sabbatical. Perhaps you like your boss, believe in the company you work for, or simply want the security of a job to return to.

If you offer your workplace value, your boss will probably want to retain you. It is generally a much more costly endeavor to replace someone than retaining someone. Still, expecting the Human Resources (HR) department to change its process can be tricky. As such, you'll need to sell your boss or the HR department on the idea. Hopefully, it won't be too much of a challenge to convince them. In the 2011 paper, *Nursing sabbatical in the acute care setting: what is the evidence?*, the authors identified the following as benefits to sabbaticals, so be sure to bring them up in your meeting or proposal.

THE PLANNING

Burnout avoidance

We touched on burnout earlier in the book. It is a type of physical, mental, or emotional exhaustion you can experience for a variety of reasons. Burnout is well documented as one of the reasons people quit their jobs. You can mention to your employer that encouraging people to take a sabbatical after a number of years of employment is a great way for the company to retain effective and productive employees.

Productivity

Mention to your employer that employees can lose their motivation and productivity for many reasons, but it is well documented that productivity increases after an employee's return from a sabbatical.

Loyalty

It has been found that employees show increased loyalty to their organizations when they are granted sabbaticals.

When trying to sell this idea to your boss, do it with your fellow employees in mind. Also, keep in mind how the business will benefit from happier, more engaged employees. In other words, convince your employer that this should be a policy change for the entire business or organization, not just for you.

Of course, you'll be the first to benefit if you succeed, but your employer will remember how forward-thinking you are and how you carry the best interests of everyone in the business at heart, and that can go a long way for you.

WHAT TO DO AFTER MY SABBATICAL?

The Short:

Just like it is wise to plan your sabbatical before it starts, it is wise to set aside time during the last part of your sabbatical to make plans for re-entering the workforce.

The Long:

Whether you choose a fixed date to end your sabbatical or go for an open-ended one, you'll have to re-enter the workforce when it ends. If you have a job to return to, your planning will be quick and mostly revolve around getting your mindset back into 'work mode.' If you're going job hunting when your sabbatical is over, you have to plan accordingly. Either way, I suggest you consider how much time you'll need after your sabbatical to get ready to re-enter the workforce.

It's best to treat these considerations as part of your sabbatical planning stage. If you have to go job hunting, schedule time into the last weeks of your sabbatical to do so. For some, looking for work and going through all the processes it involves is an emotional and stressful time, so it's best to be prepared.

Since there are many blogs, books, podcasts, and similar platforms that talk about job hunting, I encourage you to consult those if you need detailed information on how to approach the subject. Below, I'll share my own job-hunting process, as I have never come across it on other platforms. Feel free to use it as inspiration for your own process.

Note: I adapted the information below from a blog post I wrote a few years ago.

THE PLANNING 43

A while ago, I was back on the job hunting grind. I was kind of bummed about the whole experience. Something about going through websites, finding a job I'm qualified for, and applying for it was bothering me. (I later realized it was the lack of a structured system.)

A friend suggested, "Why don't you find all the jobs the way I found the truck I bought?"

While turning that over in my head, I remembered an Insanity Wolf meme, which I can't find for the life of me. Anyway, it said something like, "Goes to job interview. Interviews job."

These two ideas changed my approach to (and perception of) job hunting and, which started me on a new process. Here are the steps I learned to use:

1. *Create a list of every job-hunting, head-hunter, and corporate HR website I can think of. (I use Google docs for the entire process.)*
2. *Go through each website and copy each job for which I am remotely a fit into a separate document. As you go through step 2, you will probably find more websites that offer job opportunities, so be sure to go back to step 1 to add them.*
3. *Some companies don't disclose everything they offer in their job postings. Things like benefits or company culture can be on the company's website, as these apply to all job openings. Be sure to do your homework on all aspects that matter to you before you apply. If you can't see the information you're looking for on the companies' websites, Glassdoor is a decent resource with information on the benefits offered by many companies.*
4. *Analyze your list of opportunities to make sure you have noted everything relevant to the job offerings. You want to compare oranges to oranges.*

Things I look for include:

- *Benefits*
- *Corporate culture*
- *Time off and vacations*
- *Education budget*
- *Location*
- *Office Specifics like whether it has an open floor plan, gym, kitchen, and so on*
- *Other perks like fresh fruit, beer, or training*

1. *When you have finished steps 1 to 4, go through each document and highlight things you like in one color and things you dislike in another color.*
2. *After highlighting each page, do a plus-minus exercise. Count the occurrences of each color and write the things you liked with a plus sign and things you disliked with a minus sign. For example, +2/-4.*
3. *Rate the jobs by the plus-minus totals. If you have two with the same total, a higher minus goes under or a larger plus goes over.*
4. *Optional:*

Read the companies' Glassdoor and LinkedIn reviews. If you like what people are saying (or not) add a +1 or -1, respectively.

Congratulations! You now have every job in your area, for which you are eligible, rated from best to worst.

Now, it's just a matter of working your way through the list and mindlessly applying for jobs.

For steps 4 to 7, I printed out the jobs and used physical copies to complete the steps. It's completely possible to do this with electronic copies. However, having the print-outs made it seem more real in my mind. I must say, having a nice little stack of papers to look at made the situation seem much more hopeful and positive.

After completing this process, I also found that every day, week, or month I looked for new jobs, the search time reduced significantly. Any new option immediately jumped out from among the others I had seen many times before.

HOW DO I ACCOUNT FOR THE GAP IN MY RESUME?

The gap in my resume weighed disproportionally on my mind as my first sabbatical drew to a close. Often, I found myself wondering, "What do I write on my resume?" or, "What do I say when they ask me about it?"

However, it really doesn't look or sound as bad as it feels. It is as simple as indicating what you were up to between the time you last worked and now. I will say that, as a hiring manager, it is much better to be proactive and account for your time away from work than to leave the hiring manager wondering.

When I came back from my last sabbatical, I updated my resume with a short and sweet indication of my activities while I didn't work:

- *2017-2018 - Sabbatical*

What do I say about my sabbatical in an interview?

From all of the interviews I went to, I can recall being asked about it once. However, from the questions and overall conversation, it seemed the interviewer was less interested in my commitment to the new job and more interested in how he could take a sabbatical.

That being said, I always prepare myself to talk about my sabbatical during an interview. For example, I can talk about how I believe travel is another form of education, the personal projects I get into during my sabbaticals, and so on. (But, apart from that one interviewer being interested in taking a sabbatical, I have never actually been asked about my personal experiences during my sabbaticals. Of course, your situation may turn out different during an interview.)

If you have undertaken formal education during your sabbatical to change your career paths, this is all irrelevant. In that case, it is best to highlight your education and start your new career.

WHAT IF SOMETHING GOES WRONG DURING MY SABBATICAL?

The Short:

It's best to be prepared for unexpected situations by having a contingency plan in place. Consider the possibility of a sudden health problem or financial crisis. While these are not fun thoughts, you'll thank yourself for thinking ahead IF something drastic happens.

The Long:

There is a saying that while you're making other plans, life happens. This is so true, as even the best plans can get interrupted. As a seasoned travel sabbatee, I am very familiar with the fact that there are almost endless variables that can influence any sabbatical. While no one can foresee every possible hiccup that may occur, it is possible to have contingency plans in place. Most unexpected situations on a sabbatical will fall into two categories:

1. Health issues
2. Financial problems

Health Issues

No matter how much we hate getting sick or injured, it is inevitable and a part of the human condition.

While picking pears on my Australian backpacking adventure, a faulty ladder rung broke while I was climbing down. The fall hurt my back pretty badly, and I was laid up for weeks.

More recently, during a visa run from Thailand to Bali, I got terrible food poisoning, which led to a secondary stomach virus. After that, it took me months to heal 100 percent.

Health issues during any sabbatical will essentially translate into financial issues, but having an insurance plan in place can take care of that. Only if a larger issue pops up, you might be forced to return to your home country's health care system. If you don't plan on traveling during your sabbatical, you can continue relying on your country's health care system without extra insurance. If you are going to travel, however, definitely invest in travel insurance. For me, buying last minute medical insurance on a trip to Las Vegas saved me a whopping $8,000 (USD) hospital bill, while my friend, who did the same, saved $230,000 (USD).

Financial problems

Depending on the type of sabbatical you take, financial problems can present themselves in any number of ways.

For example, on a travel sabbatical, your passport could get stolen. In that case, you will have to get to a consulate, pay the fees for a new passport, and stay around there until the consulate issues a new passport.

Perhaps, on a sailing sabbatical, the boat might experience mechanical issues that require dry docking and an unplanned stay in a hotel.

Possibly, while backpacking through South East Asia, your backpack might get stolen from the luggage area of the bus you are traveling on.

Or, even if you stay home for your sabbatical, various things can go wrong. Your roof can start leaking, your car can break down, or flooding might happen in your area.

The above scenarios, and many more, can be mitigated with insurance and having a few extra months' worth of money available for those unexpected expenses.

Aside from health insurance, it's a case-by-case decision on which type of insurance you'd like to have during your sabbatical. There are various things to consider, like whether you need trip cancellation insurance on your flight. If your belongings get stolen, will it be cheaper just to replace them? While you cannot think of everything that could happen, it might be worth your while to write down possible scenarios and draw up a plan to be prepared for them.

Whatever your plans, I believe having enough money for a few extra months of expenses is not optional when taking a sabbatical. Furthermore, as a side note to the above discussion, consider how you will keep your money during your sabbatical. For example, if you have it parked in Exchange-Traded Funds (ETFs) in the stock market, would a downturn affect the length of your sabbatical?

While all these considerations sound a little gloomy, they really should not deter you from taking a sabbatical and having the time of your life. The benefits outweigh the risks by a long shot.

Just be prepared for the good and the bad, as this will give you peace of mind from the very start, anyway.

THE ACTION

> *An idea that is developed and put into action is more important than an idea that exists only as an idea.*
>
> EDWARD DE BONO

GO FOR IT

The Short:

This is probably the hardest chapter in the book. But it's also the shortest. Words of encouragement are just that: words. The actions, grit, fortitude and drive to take action are in your hands alone.

The Long:

Every single sabbatical I've taken has been scary to start. Whether it was boarding a plane for the Great Unknown or shedding the security blanket of a job and steady income, it has never been easy. All too easily, those daunting questions slip in:

- "Will I get another job?"

- "Do I have enough money?"
- "Did I miss something?"

Before you know it, analysis paralysis creeps in. This is when you need to trust yourself, trust in your planning, and just take the leap toward your bright and beautiful future.

 Nothing worth having comes easy.

THEODORE ROOSEVELT

Trust me, you've got this.

THE GROWTH

 All good things must come to an end.

GEOFFREY CHAUCER

WHAT DOES LIFE LOOK LIKE AFTER A SABBATICAL?

The Short:

It comes with ups and downs, but you'll go back to 'normal' a changed person.

The Long:

For most of us, the end of a sabbatical means getting back to work. It will be time to go back to your employer, time to find a new job, or time to start a new career.

One thing that surprised me when I went back to work after my last sabbatical was how much I looked forward to it. I realized I had missed the camaraderie of working with my coworkers, the challenging and unique problems I had to solve as part of my job, and even the structure of my workdays. All of this, together with other factors, influenced and reframed my thinking about my job. I went from the drudgery of day-to-day existence for a paycheck to actually looking forward to work.

There is a darker side to going back to work, which I fell prey to once: depression. Depression is a symptom of some psychological need not being met. If this happens to you, it helps to think about why you are feeling blue.

For me, I found I hadn't spent time traveling on my sabbatical, nor did I recharge before starting work again. For others, it could be a longing for the places they had been to (Scott, 2010). The problem could also be a deep unhappiness in your work. Whatever the cause behind your lack of motivation to face each day, you must try to identify it. If you can do that, you'll be in the best position to do something about it. It might even be worth your while to ask a mental healthcare professional for help.

Going back to your normal life after a sabbatical comes with good and bad consequences, but it's still something worth experiencing. Above all, it changes you and helps you grow in your personal and professional life. For me, and for most other sabbatees I have had contact with, the bad consequences are always temporary. There are many long-lasting values and positive aspects to going back to normal life after a sabbatical. It was probably best said by Scott Friedman in his paper, *A Sabbatical: The Gift That Keeps on Giving*, "The opportunity to step away from the grind of real life and explore new questions, a new culture (scientific and otherwise), and spend quality time in sharing memorable experiences with one's family is a priceless gift."

In the same paper, he notes other proven benefits:

- Your sense of wellbeing can increase consistently.

- You learn to be more resilient and not stress as much over the loss of financial resources.
- Taking sabbaticals can have positive and lasting effects on your family.

Friedman also notes the importance of enriching the people you know and interact with the experience you gained from your sabbatical. However, I believe this happens naturally and requires no real effort from your side, as simply sharing a story of what happened during your sabbatical may inspire someone else without you even knowing it.

CONSIDERATIONS

As I mentioned in the section on sleep hygiene, one of the great benefits I discovered in my sabbaticals was the chance to reset the programming in my mind from the work schedule I normally adhere to. For example, I was able to deprogram the feeling of dread I used to experience before bedtime. For many people, that feeling of dread comes from the sound of their alarm clocks ringing in the morning. Where the mind usually associates it with "time to get up for work," it can be taught to associate it with "time to get up for fun!"

When you enter your sabbatical period, you'll decouple from the "Monday to Friday, nine-to-five" mentality. In the process, you might notice behaviors in yourself that you want to change. Your sabbatical is the best time to do just that and to form new, positive, lasting habits.

Your sabbatical can also bring unexpected gifts. While on my sabbatical, I noticed old memories from my youth popping back for a visit. Sometimes, it would be events I hadn't thought about since it occurred, and often it would be a cherished memory. I believe this was the result of not having work occupying my mind from the moment I woke up to the moment I went to bed. My mind finally had the space to reflect on other things I enjoyed or needed at the time.

Pace yourself when your sabbatical starts, especially if you stay home during the first weeks (or the entire time). At the beginning of my 2014 sabbatical, it was a bit like Spring break. Excited to be free from work, I was tearing around to meet with friends to socialize and party. It was a lot of fun, but it was tiring and took time to recover. I should have scheduled a few more breaks to get used to the downtime. After a while, my friends had their lives to get back to, which led to a big gap in socializing for me. This was helpful, as it gave me time to recover and get into a sabbatical head space. Still, I think I could have paced the whole thing better and enjoyed it more if I had not pushed myself so hard.

YOUR QUICK SABBATICAL ESCAPE PLAN

Use the following questions as guidelines to start drawing up your sabbatical plans. The idea is that you turn the desire to take a sabbatical into a concrete, working plan. In time, you'll refine this outline and build on it to make your dream of taking a sabbatical a reality.

Don't just think about these questions and your answers, write them down somewhere and refer back to them as often as you can.

- Am I burned out?
- If I am burned out, what could be the causes?
- Can I realistically take a sabbatical in the next year or two?
- Will it impact my career negatively if I take a sabbatical?
- How can I convince my employer that sabbaticals are an excellent idea?
- How long should my sabbatical be?

- Can I take an open-ended sabbatical, or should it have a fixed length?
- When should I take a sabbatical?
- Consider your financial situation.
- Consider a fixed cycle, like every five years.
- How much will it cost?
- How will I pay for it?
- What will I do with my stuff?
- What am I going to do during my sabbatical?
- How will I handle a health issue if it comes up?
- How will I handle an unforeseen financial problem?
- What will I do after my sabbatical?
- Consider whether you want to stay on in your current job.
- Consider whether you are interested in a new career.
- How will I account for the gap in my resume?
- What will I say about my sabbatical in an interview?

MY LATEST SABBATICAL STORY

I've chosen to put this at the end of the book to keep the focus on the more pragmatic parts of taking a sabbatical. With any topic, I believe it's good to read up on other people's experiences to gain more insight, so I've included my story on my last sabbatical.

EUROPE

In order to talk about my latest sabbatical, I have to take you back to my second sabbatical, as they are directly related. In September 2014, I left my job. I had been working in the tech sector for 16 years, of which the last three were in the Video game industry. To say the least, I was burned out and needed a break. So, I took one.

I spent the following eight months sleeping in, cooking, exploring the city, catching up with friends and family, and doing whatever my heart desired. It was wonderful. At the end of the eight months, I re-entered the workforce and realized I had made a mistake within six months of returning. I was still burned out on my career and felt as if I had never taken a break. That's when the idea of a longer, more radical sabbatical took shape in my mind.

After thinking about it for two years, I realized the thing I craved most was an adventure to reboot myself. I also realized, looking at the list of places I wanted to travel to, it was impossible to see them all at a rate of one destination per vacation. Besides, even with the places I had visited, my list was growing much faster than it was shrinking.

I needed a travel sabbatical.

After that, all my efforts went into working out the logistics of taking time to travel. Thankfully, I had enough savings to help me sustain a travel sabbatical, and I had figured out the broad strokes of where to go, thanks to my lifelong love for traveling. The big questions I had to answer revolved around what to do with my stuff, my car, and my apartment.

Answering those questions did not take very long. I have a minimalist streak and the more I thought about it, the more it came to the forefront. Despite having a minimalist streak, the solution I was contemplating terrified me. However, it slowly grew on me until I made the decision… I would get rid of almost all of my possessions. I spent a year selling everything until all I had left was a backpack full of clothes and a box full of old coins and tax documents.

In the spring of 2017, I left to travel through Europe for a year. I had decided on Europe, as it contained the highest density of places on my list I wanted to see. Also, I had always wanted to visit all of those tiny countries, like Liechtenstein and Andorra.

I obtained a one-year holiday visa from the French government, which put a clock on my time in Europe. This was perfectly fine for me. As a Canadian, by Schengen rules, I can be in Europe for

MY LATEST SABBATICAL STORY   61

90 days in any 180-day period. So, I could roughly stay in Europe for 180 days and another 180 days in France. In hindsight, I probably wouldn't have gone with this visa. Rather, I would have spent six months of the year in non-Schengen countries. Of course, hindsight is always 20/20. But it all worked out great in any case.

With my visa process started, I landed in Paris and set about finalizing the visa application process, which ended up taking three calendar months. Rather than give you a blow by blow of my travels, I'll share the highlights.

In 2017, I managed to visit 24 countries in Europe and 60 cities and towns within those countries. In the middle of this European adventure, I took side trips to both Malaysia and Morocco.

Here are some things that stood out from this adventure:

- Beheld the treasures of the Vatican, Seville, Paris, London, San Marino, Athens, Rome, Florence, Milan, Venice and on and on and on.
- Lived the tapas lifestyle in Granada.
- Visited my great grandfather's resting place in Northern France.
- I was in London during the Westminster Bridge terror attack.
- Stumbled into protests in Paris and Barcelona.
- Ate a cornucopia of new and wondrous foods.
- Drove on the left side of the road in London rush hour traffic with a terrible hangover.
- Watched the Acropolis of Athens from a rooftop bar as it got struck by lightning.
- Partied in the Roman Pride parade.
- Reveled in the Goodwood Festival of Speed.

Here is a breakdown of the inter-city and inter-country travel methods I took in 2017:

- Train: 35
- Bus: 34
- Plane: 21
- Car: 11
- Ferry: 6
- Bicycle: 6
- There were many more car, bus, and train rides on public transit or via Uber and Grab, but I didn't count them here.

That totals 114 inter-city or inter-country trips. That works out to travel every 3.2 days. A few were day trips, but they were few and far between.

Also, I crossed one border on bicycle, one border by public transit, and one border on foot. Having my passport checked on a public transit bus was a first!

From my Australian backpacking days, I remember a cool phenomenon I call 'road friends.' When traveling from town to town, living out of a backpack and sleeping in hostels, you naturally meet fellow travelers. There is always an unspoken understanding that you are both there for a short time. Perhaps because of this fact, you tend to establish openness and trust with each other rather quickly. This allows for working together and sharing adventures.

While staying in a hostel in Paris, my roommate asked if I wanted to join him and a woman in another room for a drink at some bar near Notre Dam. I agreed, and we arranged to meet in front of the hostel in a few minutes. While waiting for them, I started chatting with another guy who was smoking. I shared our plan and asked if he wanted to join, to which he agreed. The four of us set off for adventure and ended up enjoying more adventures the following nights until we all peeled off one by one.

Time and time again, I've shared contact information with my road-friends and vice versa. Except for a few cases, we never reconnect. Perhaps it is all part of the beauty of these unique but fleeting friendships.

THAILAND

At the end of my French visa period, I headed back to Vancouver for Christmas, totally exhausted from the road, as the pace I had set was quite tiring. I was always taking in some wondrous site, having some kind of adventure, or researching and planning the next few weeks of travel. Realizing this helped me plan better for what I wanted to do next.

Exhausted as I felt, I was not finished with my traveling adventure yet. Although I still had some funds left over, it was quite low. If I wanted my money to stretch farther, I needed to travel some place with lower living costs. From the side trip I took to Malaysia while tearing through Europe, I knew the cost of living was much lower in South East Asia than in Europe. I absolutely loved my time in Malaysia, so I was eager to go somewhere else in Asia.

By then, I had also heard about the Digital Nomad movement online and on the road. This was the final piece of the puzzle. I had some financial runway, so I figured I'd give this a try and head for one of the places touted as a Digital Nomad mecca: Chiang Mai in Thailand.

After spending Christmas in Vancouver, I set off for Chiang Mai via Bangkok. Chiang Mai was an absolute blast. I really enjoyed my time there. Digital Nomadism, not not so much. While Chiang Mai is a wonderful city for Nomads, with tons of coworking spaces available, I didn't have much success launching my own Digital Nomad lifestyle. Most of my days were spent hunting down and applying for contracts. When I wasn't completing work for the few contracts I had landed, I was developing my coding skills on a personal project. Rinse and repeat... While the lifestyle is not for me, I am happy that I tried it. You, too, should try new things to determine first-hand what works (or doesn't work) for you.

One of the quirks of staying in Thailand for extended periods is doing 'border runs.' Thailand offers visas on arrival for people from many countries, valid for 30 days. During those 30 days, you can apply to extend your visa for another 30 days. This entails presenting identity documentation, proof of where you are staying, pictures of you, bank statements, and 1900 Baht (more or less $80 Canadian dollars) to a customs officer. To do that, you have to line up before the office opens and sit in a room for a long while. Not exactly a fun day.

The alternative is to leave the country and re-enter it to get another visa on arrival. This does come with some risk, and I have heard of people who were refused re-entry into Thailand after taking this route too many times. The Thai government feels, rightly so, that this is circumventing their system, so they have started clamping down a bit. Most of these stories are from people who have taken the 'border run buses' on day trips. Seeing as I wasn't a broke backpacker and that I could get cheap flights, I opted to fly to other countries for my border runs.

In March 2018, I did a border run to Bali so I could visit a friend. He and a friend of his had villas in Ubud. My friend's friend was leaving for Singapore a couple weeks early, so I was able to take over staying in his villa, gratis.

The trip was a ton of fun. Until it wasn't.

Between lounging near the pool and meeting up with more friends, I rented a scooter, and we chased around the island. We visited the rice terraces, tried Kopi luwak, and relaxed at the Jungle Fish pool bar.

One evening, we went to dinner and I ordered a swordfish dish, which gave me food poisoning and a terrible histamine reaction. I won't show you a photo, but my skin turned bright red and my eyes went bloodshot. Fortunately, we had some antihistamine pills that calmed my system a bit. I was okay the next day, but very exhausted. However, being run down, I caught a terrible stomach bug and ended up sick for the rest of my stay in Bali, which would be a few more weeks. In the end, it was months until I was over it.

In June 2018, I did another border run to Ho Chi Minh City in Vietnam. It was a pretty mild trip in comparison with others, as I was still suffering from the stomach virus I had caught in Bali. I spent a few days exploring and seeing things like the War Remnants Museum, Notre Dame, and Backpacker street, but my heart wasn't really in it.

Eventually, I was running out of money. My attempt at Digital Nomadism resulted in tiny contracts that were nowhere near enough to cover my traveling and living costs. If I were to try something like that again, I would probably secure a long-term contract first. Finances, along with the boredom of my daily Digital Nomad grind, prompted me to re-enter the workforce.

And with that, I flew to Vancouver for the summer and started job hunting.

CONCLUSION

No matter your profession, taking a sabbatical is possible when you have a solid plan in place to make it a reality. And whether you stay at home to pursue personal goals, further your education, go on a travel adventure, or realize your dream of making the world a better place by volunteering, it is an experience that will forever enrich your life.

As you continue your research into sabbaticals and start making plans to take one, always remember that a sabbatical is whatever *you* want it to be. Don't let anyone tell you otherwise.

Your daily life is, for the most part, already governed by formulas, rules, and expectations from others. Sabbaticals are different —they are your escape from the mundaneness of your everyday life and are best enjoyed when you let every day come to you with its own surprises, speed bumps, and joyous moments.

While it is wise to learn from the experiences of former and fellow sabbatees, you should be in total control of why and how you take your sabbatical. That said, you'll definitely get the most value out of your sabbatical if you plan well ahead. Yes, things

68 CONCLUSION

will go wrong along the way and everything will not happen according to your plan. However, having a plan in place will help you make the most of your free time and help you keep track of the fuel you need to sustain your break: money.

Finally, when it's time to return to your normal life, you will do so with a fresh perspective on how you want to continue your life's journey with regard to your career and personal goals, and your stories will inspire those around you.

 You are never too old to set another goal or to dream a new dream.

MALALA YOUSAFZAI

Resting my road-weary feet on the Cote d'Azur

BIBLIOGRAPHY

- Altmann, S., & Kröll, C. (2018). Understanding employees' intention to take sabbaticals. *Personnel Review*, 47(4), 882–899. https://doi.org/10.1108/pr-01-2017-0021
- Baldwin, W. (2018). Chef's sabbatical: An analysis of chef's gastronomic research through culinary tourism. *International Journal of Gastronomy and Food Science*, 13, 65–72. https://doi.org/10.1016/j.ijgfs.2018.05.006
- Bennett, H. G., & Scroggs, S. (1932). Sabbatical Leave. *The Journal of Higher Education*, 3(4), 196. https://doi.org/10.2307/1974516
- Benshoff, J. M., & Spruill, D. A. (2002). Sabbaticals for Counselor Educators: Purposes, Benefits, and Outcomes. *Counselor Education and Supervision*, 42(2), 131–144. https://doi.org/10.1002/j.1556-6978.2002.tb01805.x
- Brazeau, G. A., & van Tyle, J. H. (2006). Sabbaticals: The Key to Sharpening our Professional Skills as Educators, Scientists, and Clinicians. *American Journal of Pharmaceutical Education*, 70(5), 109. https://doi.org/10.5688/aj7005109
- Burke, E. M. (1990). A Year in Germany: A Sabbatical Dream. *The English Journal*, 79(4), 67. https://doi.org/10.2307/818133
- Burkus, D. (2017, August 10). Research Shows That Organizations Benefit When Employees Take Sabbaticals. *Harvard Business Review*. Retrieved July 9, 2022, from https://hbr.org/2017/08/research-shows-that-organizations-benefit-when-employees-take-sabbaticals
- Burnett, B., & Evans, D. (2016). *Designing Your Life: How to Build a Well-Lived, Joyful Life* (Illustrated ed.). Knopf.
- Carr, A. E., & Tang, T. L.-P. (2005). Sabbaticals and Employee Motivation: Benefits, Concerns, and Implications. *Journal of Education for Business*, 80(3), 160–164. https://doi.org/10.3200/joeb.80.3.160-164

BIBLIOGRAPHY

- M. Carraher, S., M. Crocitto, M., & Sullivan, S. (2014). A kaleidoscope career perspective on faculty sabbaticals. *Career Development International*, 19(3), 295–313. https://doi.org/10.1108/cdi-04-2013-0051
- Clements, D., & Gignac, T. (2007). *Escape 101: The Four Secrets to Taking a Sabbatical or Career Break Without Losing Your Money or Your Mind*. The Brain Ranch.
- Clevers, H., Firestein, S., Ringrose, L., Bernards, R., Darwin, K. H., & Vance, R. E. (2015). Radical Sabbaticals. *Cell*, 163(4), 788–789. https://doi.org/10.1016/j.cell.2015.10.058
- Davidson, O. B., Eden, D., Westman, M., Cohen-Charash, Y., Hammer, L. B., Kluger, A. N., Krausz, M., Maslach, C., O'Driscoll, M., Perrewé, P. L., Quick, J. C., Rosenblatt, Z., & Spector, P. E. (2010). Sabbatical leave: Who gains and how much? *Journal of Applied Psychology*, 95(5), 953–964. https://doi.org/10.1037/a0020068
- Deamer, D. W. (2011). Sabbaticals, Self-Assembly, and Astrobiology. *Astrobiology*, 11(6), 493–498. https://doi.org/10.1089/ast.2011.0632
- Demers, J. (2015, March 25). *10 Signs You're Headed For Burnout*. Inc.Africa. Retrieved July 9, 2022, from https://incafrica.com/library/jayson-demers-10-signs-you-re-headed-for-burnout
- Dlugozima, H., Scott, J., & Sharp, D. (1996). SIX MONTHS OFF: How To Plan, Negotiate, & Take The Break You Need Without Burning Bridges Or Going Broke (First Edition, first Printing ed.). Holt Paperbacks.
- Eells, W. C. (1962). The Origin and Early History of Sabbatical Leave. AAUP Bulletin, 48(3), 253. https://doi.org/10.2307/40222893
- Fannin, R. A., & Lee, K. (2011). *Startup Asia: Top Strategies for Cashing in on Asia's Innovation Boom* (1st ed.). Wiley.
- Ferriss, T. (2007). *The 4-Hour Work Week*. Macmillan Publishers.
- Franks, J., Chenhall, R., & Keogh, L. (2018). The Facebook Sabbatical as a Cycle: Describing the Gendered Experience of Young Adults as They Navigate Disconnection and Reconnection.

Social Media + Society, 4(3), 205630511880199. https://doi.org/10.1177/2056305118801995
- Friedman S. L. (2018). A Sabbatical: The Gift That Keeps on Giving. *Cellular and molecular gastroenterology and hepatology*, 5(4), 656–658. https://doi.org/10.1016/j.jcmgh.2018.01.010
- Gaziel, H. H. (1995). Sabbatical leave, job burnout and turnover intentions among teachers. *International Journal of Lifelong Education*, 14(4), 331–338. https://doi.org/10.1080/0260137950140406
- Genty, P. (2000). *Clients Don't Take Sabbaticals: The Indispensable In-House Clinic and the Teaching of Empathy*. Scholarship Archive. Retrieved July 9, 2022, from https://scholarship.law.columbia.edu/faculty_scholarship/1048/
- Gernon T. (2020). A sabbatical reboot. *Science* (New York, N.Y.), 370(6517), 738. https://doi.org/10.1126/science.370.6517.738
- Goldberg, T. (1988). An Academic in Practice—or—How about a Sabbatical Doing Social Work? *Journal of Social Work Education*, 24(3), 211–220. https://doi.org/10.1080/10437797.1988.10671255
- Graffeo, C. S., Parney, I. F., Wessel, B. L., & Spinner, R. J. (2020). In Reply to the Letter to the Editor Regarding "A Surprise Sabbatical: How Mayo Clinic Neurosurgery Coped with COVID-19." *World Neurosurgery*, 144, 330. https://doi.org/10.1016/j.wneu.2020.09.020
- Guillebeau, C. (2010). *The Art of Non-Conformity: Set Your Own Rules, Live the Life You Want, and Change the World (Perigee Book.)* (8.8.2010 ed.). TarcherPerigee.
- Haymarket Business Interactive, & Garrett, A. (2008, July 8). *Crash Course in: Offering sabbaticals - Management Today*. Haymarket Publishing. Retrieved July 9, 2022, from https://web.archive.org/web/20100626013527/http://www.managementtoday.co.uk/search/article/831180/crash-course-in-offering-sabbaticals/
- Higuera, V. (2017, March 29). *5 Signs You're Headed for Burnout at Work, and What You Can Do to Fix It*. Healthline. Retrieved July 9, 2022, from https://www.healthline.com/health/signs-you-are-headed-for-a-burnout-at-work

BIBLIOGRAPHY

- Honig, B. (2018). Is Man a "Sabbatical Animal"? Agamben, Rosenzweig, Heschel, Arendt. *Political Theology*, 20(1), 1–23. https://doi.org/10.1080/1462317x.2018.1518766
- How Gambling Saved Me From a Misspent Sabbatical. (1977). *Journal of Humanistic Psychology*, 17(3), 19–34. https://doi.org/10.1177/002216787701700303
- Hubbard, M. (2002). Exploring the Sabbatical or Other Leave as a Means of Energizing a Career, *The Free Library*. https://www.thefreelibrary.com/Exploring the sabbatical or other leave as a means of energizing a...-a090219521
- Intel. (n.d.). *Choose Your Own Adventure with the Intel Sabbatical*. Retrieved July 9, 2022, from https://www.intel.com/content/www/us/en/jobs/videos/choose-own-adventure-sabbatical-video.html
- Iravania, H. (2011). Analyzing impacts of sabbatical leaves of absence regarding faculty members, University of Tehran. *Procedia - Social and Behavioral Sciences*, 15, 3608–3615. https://doi.org/10.1016/j.sbspro.2011.04.343
- Monster, & Isaacs, K. (2022, April 5). *Explain Your Sabbatical on Your Resume*. Monster Career Advice. Retrieved July 9, 2022, from https://www.monster.com/career-advice/article/explain-sabbatical-on-your-resume
- Jarecky, R. K., & Sandifer, M. G. (1986). Faculty members' evaluations of sabbaticals. Academic Medicine, 61(10), 803–807. https://doi.org/10.1097/00001888-198610000-00004
- Johnson, A. M. (2018). Librarian sabbaticals: Overcoming the hurdles and realizing the benefits. College & Research Libraries News, 79(11), 607. https://doi.org/10.5860/crln.79.11.607
- Kang, B., & Miller, M. T. (1999). *An Overview of the Sabbatical Leave in Higher Education: A Synopsis of the Literature Base*. (ED430471) ERIC Institute of Education Sciences. https://files.eric.ed.gov/fulltext/ED430471.pdf
- Kimball, B. A. (1978). The Origin of the Sabbath and Its Legacy to the Modern Sabbatical. *The Journal of Higher Education*, 49(4), 303. https://doi.org/10.2307/1979188

BIBLIOGRAPHY

- Krantz, W.B. (2009). *Sabbaticals And Academic Leaves: An Investment In Your Future!*
- Kraus, P. L. (2018). A Primer on Librarians Sabbaticals: A Case Study of a Six-Month Sabbatical at Home and Abroad. *Journal of Religious & Theological Information*, 17(4), 121–127. https://doi.org/10.1080/10477845.2018.1446700
- Kukreti, R. (2007, August 9). *Portrait of a partnership.* Business Today. Retrieved July 9, 2022, from https://www.businesstoday.in/magazine/new-business/story/portrait-of-a-partnership-12010-2007-08-08
- McDonalds. (n.d.). *Benefits*. McDonald's Corporation. Retrieved July 9, 2022, from https://careers.mcdonalds.com/us-corporate-who-we-are-perks-benefits
- Napoletano, E., & Schmidt, J. (2021, March 25). *Top 4 Retirement Worries—And How To Handle Them*. Forbes Advisor. Retrieved July 9, 2022, from https://www.forbes.com/advisor/retirement/top-retirement-worries/
- Oxtoby, K. (2014). Are sabbaticals still an option for today's doctors? *BMJ*, g1212. https://doi.org/10.1136/bmj.g1212
- Pillinger, M. H., Lemon, S. C., Zand, M. S., Foster, P. J., Merchant, J. S., Kimberly, R., Allison, J., Cronstein, B. N., Galeano, C., Holden-Wiltse, J., Trayhan, M., White, R. J., Davin, A., & Saag, K. G. (2019). Come from away: Best practices in mini-sabbaticals for the development of young investigators: a White Paper by the SEQUIN (mini-Sabbatical Evaluation and QUality ImprovemeNt) Group. *Journal of Clinical and Translational Science*, 3(1), 37–44. https://doi.org/10.1017/cts.2019.369
- Robbins, I. P. (1987). *Judicial Sabbaticals* (No. 106352NCJRS). The Federal Judicial Center. https://www.ojp.gov/pdffiles1/Digitization/106352NCJRS.pdf
- Scott, Deborah Ann. (2019). *The Value of Sabbaticals to Revitalize and Retain Nurse Leaders in a Hospital Setting*. Retrieved from Sophia, the St. Catherine University repository website: https://sophia.stkate.edu/maol_theses/36

BIBLIOGRAPHY

- Scott, J. C. (1992). Planning and Implementing a Sabbatical Leave Abroad. *Journal of Education for Business*, 67(4), 238–242. https://doi.org/10.1080/08832323.1992.10117551
- Sima, C. M. (2000). The Role and Benefits of the Sabbatical Leave in Faculty Development and Satisfaction. *New Directions for Institutional Research*, 2000(105), 67–75. https://doi.org/10.1002/ir.10506
- Singletary, P. G. (2019, January 3). *History of Sabbaticals (from The Gift of a Sabbatical Series)*. LinkedIn. Retrieved July 9, 2022, from https://www.linkedin.com/pulse/gift-sabbatical-part-two-history-sabbaticals-g-page-singletary
- Spacht, Beth Anne, *"Perspectives on sabbaticals and job satisfaction in nonprofit organizations"* (2018). School of Professional and Continuing Studies Nonprofit Studies Capstone Projects. 1. https://scholarship.richmond.edu/spcs-nonprofitstudies-capstones/1
- Spencer, M., Clay, H., Hearne, G., & James, P. (2012). A comparative examination of the use of academic sabbaticals. T*he International Journal of Management Education*, 10(3), 147–154. https://doi.org/10.1016/j.ijme.2012.06.003
- Spencer, M., & Kent, P. (2007). Perpetuating difference? Law school sabbaticals in the era of performativity. *Legal Studies*, 27(4), 649–677. https://doi.org/10.1111/j.1748-121x.2007.00064.x
- Stelfox, H. T., Straus, S. E., & Sackett, D. L. (2015). Clinician-trialist rounds: 27. Sabbaticals. Part 2: I'm taking a sabbatical! How should I prepare for it? *Clinical Trials*, 12(3), 287–290. https://doi.org/10.1177/1740774514567970
- Straus, S. E., & Sackett, D. L. (2014). Clinician-trialist rounds: 26. Sabbaticals. Part 1: Should I take a sabbatical? *Clinical Trials*, 12(2), 174–176. https://doi.org/10.1177/1740774514562917
- Stright, I. L. (1964). Sabbatical Leave: A Critique. *The Journal of Higher Education*, 35(7), 388. https://doi.org/10.2307/1979456
- Swenty, C. F., Schaar, G. L., Phillips, L. A., Embree, J. L., McCool, I. A., & Shirey, M. R. (2011). Nursing sabbatical in the acute care setting: what is the evidence?. *Nursing forum*, 46(3), 195–204. https://doi.org/10.1111/j.1744-6198.2011.00225.x

BIBLIOGRAPHY

- Tait, I. (1987). Take a sabbatical from general practice. *BMJ*, 295(6599), 644–646. https://doi.org/10.1136/bmj.295.6599.644
- Talbott, J. A. (1995). Sabbaticals. *Academic Psychiatry*, 19(3), 159–166. https://doi.org/10.1007/bf03341427
- Thie, H. J., M.C.H., & Thibault, M. (2003). *Officer Sabbaticals: Analysis of Extended Leave Options* (No. MR1752). RAND. https://www.rand.org/content/dam/rand/pubs/monograph_reports/2005/MR1752.pdf
- Tyler, K. (2011, December 1). *Sabbaticals Pay Off*. SHRM. Retrieved July 9, 2022, from https://www.shrm.org/hr-today/news/hr-magazine/pages/1211tyler.aspx
- Way, B. (2009, December). *Giving myself a timeout*. Entrepreneurs' Organization. https://www.eonetwork.org/octane-magazine/december-2009/givingmyselfatimeout
- Webster, M. (2008, May 6). *Can You Catch Up on Lost Sleep?* Scientific American. Retrieved July 9, 2022, from https://www.scientificamerican.com/article/fact-or-fiction-can-you-catch-up-on-sleep/
- Wikipedia contributors. (2021, January 9). *Career break*. Wikipedia. https://en.wikipedia.org/wiki/Career_break
- Wikipedia contributors. (2022, June 12). *Dot-com bubble*. Wikipedia. https://en.wikipedia.org/wiki/Dot-com_bubble
- Wikipedia contributors. (2022, April 10). *Digital nomad*. Wikipedia. https://en.wikipedia.org/wiki/Digital_nomad
- Wikipedia contributors. (2022, May 14). *FIRE movement*. Wikipedia. https://en.wikipedia.org/wiki/FIRE_movement
- Wikipedia contributors. (2022, July 8). *Gap year*. Wikipedia. https://en.wikipedia.org/wiki/Gap_year
- Wikipedia contributors. (2022, June 9). *Otium*. Wikipedia. https://en.wikipedia.org/wiki/Otium
- Wikipedia contributors. (2022, June 24). *Sabbatical*. Wikipedia. https://en.wikipedia.org/wiki/Sabbatical
- Wikipedia contributors. (2022, February 12). *Transformative learning*. Wikipedia. https://en.wikipedia.org/wiki/Transformative_learning

BIBLIOGRAPHY

- Wildman, Katherine Leigh. *"Staff sabbaticals: an examination of sabbatical purposes and benefits for higher education administrators."* PhD (Doctor of Philosophy) thesis, University of Iowa, 2012. http://ir.uiowa.edu/etd/3009
- Winter, C. W. (2017). *The Sleep Solution: Why Your Sleep is Broken and How to Fix It* (1st ed.). Berkley.
- Witt, L., & Ortberg, J. (2011). *Replenish: Leading From A Healthy Soul* (37534th ed.). Baker Books.
- Zahir, A. T., & Fakhri, L. (2011). Improve faculty effectiveness by sabbatical leave. *Procedia - Social and Behavioral Sciences*, 29, 917–926. https://doi.org/10.1016/j.sbspro.2011.11.322
- Zahorski, K. J. (1994). *The Sabbatical Mentor: A Practical Guide to Successful Sabbaticals*. Anker Pub Co.

ABOUT THE AUTHOR

Matthew Sawasy is an experienced sabbattee who recently discovered his passion for sharing his sabbatical experiences with others. During his last sabbatical, Matthew beheld the treasures of the Vatican, Seville, Paris, London, San Marino, Athens, Rome, Florence, Milan, Venice and on and on and on, as he traveled through 24 European countries and even squeezed Malaysia and Morocco into the mix. Among his adventures, he crossed one border on a bicycle, one using public transport, and another one on foot, all while meeting many interesting citizens of the world.

Matthew hopes to inspire aspiring sabbattees to follow their dreams and turn them into realities so they can live more fulfilled lives that overflow with fun and memorable moments to reflect on and share with their friends and loved ones.

Printed in Great Britain
by Amazon